The Pumpkin Goal

By Sally Cowan

“Wake up, kits!”
called Mum Skunk.
“Let’s go out!”

Clove jumped up.

Pete woke up with a groan.
He did not want to leave
his pillow of sticks.

No, I'm so cosy!
Clove
Pete

The skunks roamed up the hill.

The kits came to a hollow oak log.

“Chase me into this log, Clove!”
Pete called.
“Don’t be slow!”

The kits ran out of the low log.

Then the kits froze.

“It is a pumpkin!” said Mum.
“It has grown very big!”

Pete felt the pumpkin
with his toe.

"It's too big to take home,"
moaned Pete.

"I can roll it on the road,"
Clove boasted.
"Let me show you."

Let's go!

Back at home,
Mum made a hole
in the pumpkin.

Clove and Pete jumped inside
and ate loads of pumpkin!

"My goal is to eat
all of the pumpkin!" said Pete.

Clove and Pete went back in the den for a cosy nap.

The kits dreamed of rows of pumpkins.